# Buddhist

## Anita Ganeri

🐸 CHILDRENS PRESS ®

A Division of Grolier Publishing

New York  London  Hong Kong  Sydney

Danbury, Connecticut

First American Edition 1997 by
Children's Press
A Division of Grolier Publishing
Sherman Turnpike
Danbury, CT 06816

Library of Congress Cataloging in Publication Data
Ganeri, Anita. 1961-
   Buddhist / Anita Ganeri.
     p. cm. — (Beliefs and cultures)
   Includes index.
   Summary: introduces the religion of
   Buddhism, describing its origins and
   traditions. Includes related crafts and
   activities.
   ISBN 0-516-08086-5
   1. Buddhism—Juvenile literature. [1.
   Buddhism.] I. Title. II. Series.
   BQ4032.G36 1997             96-4409
   294.3—dc20                  CIP AC

Series Editor: Sarah Ridley
Copy Editor: Nicola Barber
Designer: Liz Black
Photographer (activities): Peter Millard
Illustrators: Aziz Khan page 8,
Picture Researcher: Sarah Moule
Consultants: Vishvapani of London Buddhist
Centre and Marty Casey of Clearvision Trust
Photographs: e t archive 9t; Art and Architecture
Library 11t; Bridgeman Art Library 4, 10, 14,
27b; British Museum 5t, 12b; J Allan Cash 6;
Clearvision Trust 13; Eye Ubiquitous 5b, 18b,
31bl; Robert Harding Picture Library 7t, 7b, 9b,
16t, 25b; Michael Holford 20t, 20b; Hutchison
Library 8t, 11b, 12t, 15b, 22b, 24t, 24b, 25t,
26b, 27t, 31t, 31br; Impact Photo Library 16b,
18t, 19, 22t; Panos Pictures 30t; Bury Peerless
26t; Trip 15t.

# CONTENTS

# IN THE BUDDHA'S FOOTSTEPS

About 2,500 years ago, there lived a man called Siddhartha Gautama. Siddhartha was a royal prince, and he led a life of luxury in his father's palace. But all the finery and riches around him did not make him happy, so he decided to seek the true meaning of life. After many years of searching, Siddhartha found what he was looking for - an answer to life's suffering. He became the Buddha, or "enlightened one" and spent the rest of his life preaching his message. The people who followed him and based their lives on his teachings became known as Buddhists.

The Buddha was an historical figure who lived in India some 2,500 years ago. The religion he founded is still practiced today.

## A ROYAL BIRTH

Prince Siddhartha was born in the year 623 B.C., in the village of Lumbini which today lies in Nepal. He was the son of King Suddhodana and Queen Maya. Legend has it that nine months before the prince's birth, his mother dreamed of a white elephant - a sign that her son would be an extraordinary being.

Astrologers told the king that Siddhartha would become a great ruler, or, if he saw suffering, a great religious teacher. The king wanted his son to rule after him, so he shielded him from the world by keeping him inside the family palace. Siddhartha married his cousin, Princess Yashodara, and had a son, Rahula.

The Buddha's footprint, beautifully carved in brass. The Buddha was often shown by symbols, rather than in person.

A row of golden Buddhas, in the Wat Po temple, Bangkok, Thailand. There are 394 of these statues in the temple.

## THE FOUR SIGNS

Four times, against his father's orders, Siddhartha rode in his chariot outside the palace walls. The suffering and unhappiness that he saw changed his life. First he came across an old man, then a sick man, then the body of a dead man surrounded by his grieving family. Siddhartha realized that, despite his wealthy life-style, he could not escape the effects of old age, sickness, and death. So when he came across a wandering holy man sitting by the roadside, Siddhartha decided to become like him and search for an answer to the problems of life's sufferings.

## LEAVING HOME

At the age of 29, Siddhartha left the family palace, cut off his hair, and put on beggar's robes. He spent some time in the forest, studying with two famous religious teachers. But they could not tell him what he wanted to know. Then he spent six years fasting and praying. This simply left him starving and weak. Then he came to the town of Bodh-Gaya, in India, and sat under a huge *bodhi* tree to meditate. After 49 days and

A *bodhi* tree in Sri Lanka. It was beneath a tree like this one that the Buddha sat and meditated.

49 nights, he finally gained enlightenment. He realized that people were unhappy because they were never content with what they had. They always wanted more.

## TEACHING AND TRAVELING

For the next 40 years, the Buddha traveled around India, teaching people new ways of thinking and behaving in order to be free from greed and suffering. He died, at age 80, in the town of Kushinagara in northeastern India, and entered *nirvana*, a state of perfect bliss and happiness.

The Dhamekh Stupa at Sarnath, India. The Buddha preached his first sermon at Sarnath, before traveling around India.

The Buddha died lying on his side. This huge statue in Burma shows the *parinirvana*, or the Buddha entering the state of *nirvana*.

Buddhist monks in Vietnam, wearing traditional robes. There are many Buddhists in Southeast Asia.

## SPREADING THE WORD

After gaining enlightenment, the Buddha taught his followers what he had discovered and sent them to spread his teaching, called the *dharma*, throughout India and beyond. Today, there are more than 400 million Buddhists in the world. Although the majority of Buddhists still live in Asia, Buddhism has also spread during this century to Europe, the U.S., Australia, New Zealand, and Canada.

Buddhism has spread from India to many parts of the world.

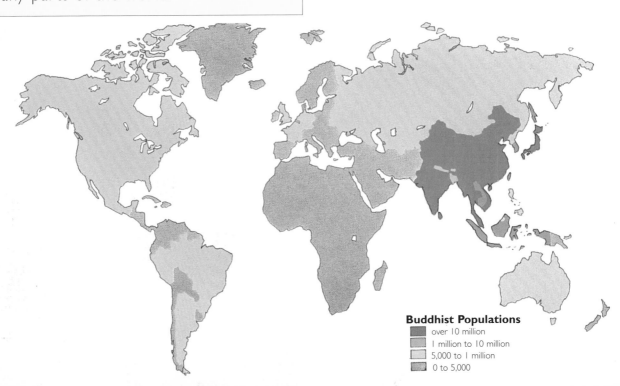

**Buddhist Populations**
- over 10 million
- 1 million to 10 million
- 5,000 to 1 million
- 0 to 5,000

## EMPEROR ASHOKA

The Buddha's teachings were spread by monks, nuns, and new converts such as the great Indian emperor, Ashoka, who reigned from 269-231 B.C. After a particularly bloody battle in which 100,000 people were killed, Ashoka was filled with remorse. He became a Buddhist and, from then on, followed the Buddhist way of peace and nonviolence. Ashoka set up stone pillars carved with Buddhist teachings throughout his empire, and sent missionaries far and wide to spread the word.

This lion sculpture once stood on top of a tall, stone pillar, built by Ashoka at Sarnath. Today, it is the symbol of the modern republic of India.

## DIFFERENT GROUPS

Some time after the Buddha's death, his followers split into different groups, or schools, depending on his different teachings. The Mahayana school of Buddhism spread its teachings to Nepal, China, Japan, Vietnam, and Korea. The Theravada school spread to Sri Lanka, Burma, Thailand, Cambodia, and Laos. The Tantric school of Buddhism spread to Tibet, Bhutan, and Mongolia.

The Buddhist Peace Pagoda in London, England. The peaceful and caring attitudes of Buddhism have attracted many people in the West.

# THE BUDDHIST PATH

The Buddha had many followers, especially among ordinary people. He taught them to follow the "Middle Path" between the extremes of luxury and hardship. The Buddha did not want to be worshiped as a god, nor did he claim that his was the only path. His teachings were simply a guide to help people lead better lives, like a raft to help travelers cross a river to the Buddha's world. Everyone had to take responsibility for themselves and try to gain enlightenment through meditation, wisdom, self-control, and helping others.

A Buddhist *thangka* painting, showing the wheel of life, held up by Yama, god of death. Inside the wheel are many different states of rebirth.

## THE FIRST SERMON

In his first sermon, at the deer park in Sarnath, India, the Buddha explained the basic points of his teaching. First, he drew a wheel on the ground. This represented the endless cycle of birth, death, and rebirth that everyone is caught up in. To break free from this cycle, and to gain enlightenment, people needed to follow the Buddha's teachings.

The Buddha and his followers traveled around India as monks, teaching people about the Four Noble Truths.

The Four Noble Truths form the first part of the Buddha's teachings:

1. Human life is full of suffering.
2. The reason for suffering is greed. People are never happy with what they have got. They always want more.
3. It is possible to find an end to suffering.
4. The way to end suffering is to follow the Middle Path.

These monks in Bhutan are blessing worshipers, just as the Buddha might have done thousands of years ago.

## THE MIDDLE PATH

The Middle Path is also called the Noble Eightfold Path. The Buddha taught that by following the eight steps of this path, people could overcome their greed and suffering and live better, wiser, more generous lives. This was the way to enlightenment. The eight steps of the Noble Eightfold Path are:

1. Right understanding - understanding the Buddha's teachings.
2. Right attitude - clear, positive thinking.
3. Right speech - speaking wisely and truthfully, not telling lies.
4. Right action - doing good for its own sake and not for reward.
5. Right livelihood - doing a job that does not harm others.
6. Right effort - trying to do good deeds, not bad ones.
7. Right thoughts - thinking before you speak or act.
8. Right meditation - developing a calm and happy mind.

## THE THREE JEWELS

The Buddha is one of the Three Jewels of Buddhism. The other two jewels are the *dharma*, or teaching of

At this shrine, Buddhists show their respect for the Buddha with offerings, and by pouring water over a statue of the Buddha.

the Buddha, and the *sangha*, or Buddhist community. All Buddhists make a commitment to these three ideals and take them as their guides through life. The Buddha is sometimes described as a doctor, the *dharma* as the medicine he prescribes, and the *sangha* as the nurse who gives the medicine to the patient.

These three wheels represent the Three Jewels of Buddhism - the Buddha, the *dharma*, and the *sangha*.

## LIVING AS A BUDDHIST

The Buddha taught his followers that the way to better understanding was to take responsibility for their own actions and to realize the truth for themselves. One way of doing this was through meditation (see page 22). Living as a Buddhist also involves following a set of guidelines, called the Five Precepts. They are:

1. Not harming or killing living things.
2. Not taking things unless they are freely given.
3. Having a sensible, decent life-style.
4. Not speaking unkindly or deceitfully.
5. Not taking drugs or drinking alcohol.

Buddhists believe that the way to find happiness is to be caring toward other people and to stop wanting things for themselves. This can sometimes be difficult, especially in Western countries where possessions are important parts of people's lives. One of the first things a Buddhist learns, wherever they are in the world, is to be kinder and more generous to others, and to live a simpler life. They learn too that meditation helps them to grow and develop the potential of oneself.

In the West, Buddhist parents teach their children to be kind to other people, as the Buddha taught.

INTERVIEW

I became a Buddhist after I learned to meditate. I found out that I could change and develop - even though I was nearly 40! I know that I can continue to grow and change by practising the Five Precepts, and meditating - especially if I am helped by my Buddhist friends.

**Marty Casey, age 49**
**Manchester, U.K.**

# MANY TRADITIONS

This *thangka* painting shows Tara, a goddess worshiped by Buddhists in Tibet.

There are many different groups of Buddhists. They all share the same belief in the Three Jewels, but follow the Buddha's different teachings, so they have different ways of practicing their faith.

## TWO VEHICLES

The two main schools of Buddhism are Theravada (the Way of the Elders) and Mahayana (the Great Vehicle). The Theravada school sticks strictly to the original teachings of the Buddha. Its followers believe that a person has full and sole responsibility for his or her own destiny. They also believe that only monks can achieve enlightenment. The Mahayana school is more flexible and encourages many different ways of thinking. Its followers believe that an individual's life and actions are closely linked to those of other people. They believe that each individual has the potential to develop and grow as a person.

## INTERVIEW

In my city, there are shrines to the Buddha everywhere you go. My mother prays every day at the shrine near our house. There are many Hindu temples too and many people follow a mixture of Hindu and Buddhist beliefs.

**Dinesh, age 16**
**Kathmandu, Nepal.**

## PERFECT BEINGS

In Mahayana Buddhism, the ideal of the perfect person, or *bodhisattva*, is very important. This is someone who has gained enlightenment but puts off reaching *nirvana* in order to help other people. A *bodhisattva* is generous, kind, patient, compassionate, and wise. These are all qualities that Buddhists try to develop for themselves.

The Potala Palace in Lhasa, Tibet, was the home of the Dalai Lama, the spiritual head of the Tibetan Buddhists.

## THE WAY OF ZEN

One of the most important types of Japanese Buddhism is called Zen, which means "contemplation." The emphasis of Zen Buddhism is to gain enlightenment directly through meditation and strict mental training, although Zen Buddhists also read sacred texts and do good works. Martial arts such as shadow boxing, paintings, and poems, and specially designed gardens are all used to help people concentrate and focus their minds. Learning to meditate properly can take many years.

Zen Buddhists create special gardens as symbols of peace and simplicity. The gardens help them to meditate.

## BUDDHISM IN THE WEST

Buddhism spread to Europe and the U.S. at the beginning of this century and is still growing in popularity. The first Buddhist temple in Britain was built in London in 1926. Apart from Westerners who have become Buddhists, many Buddhist people have moved to the West from Thailand, Burma, Tibet, Japan, Korea, and Taiwan, establishing their own temples, monasteries, and meditation schools.

## BUDDHIST TIBET

Tibetans follow a form of Buddhism known as Tantric Buddhism. They show their feelings through worship and colorful ritual. Their spiritual teachers are called *lamas*. Buddhism came to Tibet from India and China 1,300 years ago and, until recently, there were thousands of monasteries and tens of thousands of monks. But since the Chinese invasion of Tibet in 1959, many monasteries have been destroyed and many monks arrested or killed.

On special occasions, Tibetan monks perform dances and ceremonies based on important events in Buddhist history.

## OCEAN OF WISDOM

The leader of Tibet's Buddhists is called the Dalai Lama, which means "ocean of wisdom." He is believed to be the *bodhisattva* Avalokiteshvara in human form. When one Dalai Lama dies, the search begins for a baby boy to replace him. The baby must pass several tests to prove that he is the right choice. Traditionally, he is then taken to Lhasa, the capital of Tibet, to be trained. The present Dalai Lama is the 14th in line. However, he was forced to flee from Tibet after the Chinese invasion and now lives in exile in India with thousands of his followers.

The Dalai Lama lives in exile in India. He travels around the world, talking to people about Buddhism and about Tibet.

# MAKING NOODLES WITH TOFU

Most Buddhists are vegetarians. Here is a recipe to try.

*YOU WILL NEED:*

- *1 packet thread egg noodles*
- *1 tablespoon of oil*
- *8oz tofu (soya bean curd), cut into small chunks*
- *8oz mixed vegetables (for example, carrots, green or red pepper, mushrooms, spring onions), all chopped quite finely*
- *knife*   *wooden spoon*   *wok or frying pan*
- *1 teaspoon crushed root ginger*
- *3 tablespoons of soy sauce*   *bowl to serve*
- ❤ *Ask an adult to help you with this activity.*

## WHAT TO DO:

**1** You can cook the noodles in two ways. Either bring a pan of water to boil, add the noodles, and boil for another 3-4 minutes, or put the noodles in a bowl, pour on a kettleful of boiling water, and leave for 3-4 minutes. Drain.

**2** Heat the oil in a wok or deep frying pan. Add the spring onions and ginger and stir-fry for a few seconds. Add the tofu and stir-fry for 2 minutes until brown and crisp. Remove from the pan and drain on paper towels.

**3** Add the remaining vegetables to the pan and stir-fry for 4-5 minutes until cooked but still crisp. Return the tofu to the pan and pour the soy sauce over. Stir well to mix.

**4** Add the noodles to the pan and stir again. Heat thoroughly. Serve in a bowl at once.

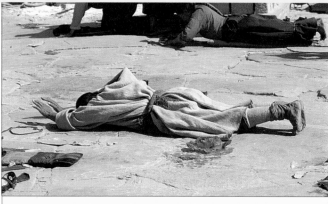

In Tibet, pilgrims lie on the ground in front of the temple to show their respect for the Buddha.

the temple they observe the Five Precepts of good behavior (see page 13), bow, and make offerings of flowers, incense, and food to a statue of the Buddha or a *bodhisattva*. They also say prayers or recite passages from the sacred books. In this way, they show their thanks and respect to the Buddha.

For Buddhists, the Middle Path is a complete way of life that they aim to follow all the time. They try to lead their lives according to the Buddha's teachings, learning to do good, and to act and think well. Many Buddhists also visit temples or shrines to honor the Buddha and to meditate with other Buddhists. Inside

**PRAYER WHEELS AND PRAYER FLAGS**

When Tibetan Buddhists visit a temple, they walk around the shrine in a clockwise direction. As they walk, they set gigantic prayer wheels spinning with their hands. Inside each wheel is a paper scroll on which hundreds of prayers are written. By spinning the wheels, the worshipers release the prayers into the world. Brightly colored flags, also printed with prayers, flutter from the top of every Tibetan temple and monastery.

By spinning each prayer wheel in turn, the prayers written inside them are able to fly to all four corners of the world.

**STUPAS AND PAGODAS**

The earliest Buddhist shrines were bell-shaped monuments called *stupas*. The first *stupas* were built as burial mounds to contain the Buddha's ashes and last possessions. Later, *stupas* were built to hold copies of the sacred texts and the ashes of important monks, and as sacred symbols. As Buddhism spread, the shape of the shrines changed. In Japan, *stupas* turned into taller, thinner pagodas.

Prayer flags flutter from the stupa of Bodhnath in Kathmandu, Nepal, while the Buddha's all-seeing eyes keep watch.

## BUDDHIST ART

The earliest types of Buddhist art showed scenes from the Buddha's life, carved in stone or painted on cave walls. The Buddha himself was not shown as a person, but represented by symbols. These included footprints, a lotus flower (see opposite page), a wheel, a *bodhi* tree, a *stupa*, and an empty throne with an umbrella held above it.

This 2nd or 3rd century Indian stone statue shows the Buddha preaching.

This exquisite thangka painting shows the eight-armed figure of the *bodhisattva*, Avalokiteshvara, surrounded by scenes from Buddhist history.

## SCULPTURES AND STATUES

Today, there are sculptures and statues of the Buddha in every Buddhist temple and monastery. Styles vary from place to place, but every statue must give out a feeling of peace. The hands of the Buddha are portrayed in different positions, called *mudras*. Each *mudra* has a special meaning. There are *mudras* to show teaching, blessings, and protection.

## SACRED THANGKAS

*Thangkas* are sacred Tibetan paintings that show the Buddha, the *bodhisattvas*, and scenes from their lives and from Buddhist history. *Thangkas* are painted on cotton or silk, following ancient rules about which shapes, patterns, and colors the artist can use.

# MAKING A LOTUS FLOWER

*YOU WILL NEED:*

• *good-quality pink and white paper*

• *green paper*     • *tape*       • *scissors*

• *thick felt-tip pen*

*(You can make several lotus flowers, in white and pink.)*

## WHAT TO DO:

**1** Cut two strips of paper, 12 x 4 inches. Fold each strip in half once, then in half again, then in half again (three times in total).

**4** Take one strip of petals and scrunch the bottom to make a flower. Stick the ends together and push into the top of the stem. Tape in place. Spread the petals out evenly. Cut the second strip into individual petals. Use tape to stick them around the outside of the first flower.

**2** Cut the petal shape from the folded paper. Unfold each strip carefully.

**3** To make the stem, cut a piece of green paper 8 x 4 inches. Roll it around the thick felt-tip pen to form a tube. Stick the ends in place. (Don't forget to remove the pen!)

**5** Use a strip of green paper to hide the white or pink band and tape under the flower.

# MEDITATION

A Western Buddhist nun meditating, an important part of being a Buddhist.

## MEDITATION

In his search for enlightenment, the Buddha meditated for 49 days and 49 nights under the *bodhi* tree at Bodh-Gaya. Meditation is very important to Buddhists. They believe that by training their minds and bringing their thoughts and feelings under control, they will gain awareness and enlightenment.

Buddhists often meditate in groups, kneeling on cushions or on stools, or sitting cross-legged on the floor. They sit very quietly, eyes closed, breathing calmly and regularly and trying to concentrate their minds on one point of their own body, only without any thoughts being in their mind. As thoughts fly into their minds, they must simply let them go again. It is not an easy thing to do!

## KEEPING IN FOCUS

Learning to meditate properly takes years of practice. Buddhists have developed many ways of clearing and calming their minds and developing positive emotions. These include chanting a simple sacred verse, called a *mantra*, over and over again. Buddhists may also concentrate on their breathing, or on an object such as a candle or a picture, to help focus their attention.

Making a *mandala* (see page 23) needs great patience and skill, as well as good eyesight.

# MAKING A MANDALA

The word *mandala* means circle. It is the name given to a special circular design used by Tibetan Buddhists to help concentrate their minds as they meditate. Monks learn to trace extremely complicated *mandalas* out of colored sand. Follow these steps to create your own *mandala*.

*YOU WILL NEED:*
- *a large sheet of white cardboard*
- *felt-tip pen*   •*colored glitter*
- *glue*

## WHAT TO DO:

**1** First you need to draw a *mandala* design on the cardboard. Start with a large circle.

**2** In the center of the circle, draw something that is important to you. This might be a flower, a star, a leaf, or another fairly simple shape. The center symbol of a *mandala* represents a special quality such as wisdom or generosity.

**3** Leave four openings around your central picture. These openings are like paths for reaching the quality at the center. Build up your *mandala* around the central picture.

**4** When your design is complete decorate it with glitter, section by section. Use different colors to represent different qualities. White is used for the Buddha's purity, red for his compassion, and blue for his teachings.

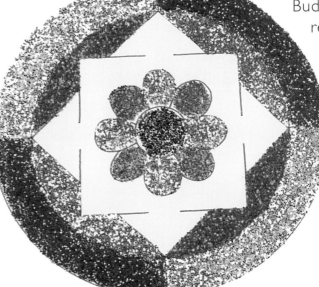

All of those who follow the teachings of the Buddha are members of the *sangha*, or Buddhist community. However, in Theravadin Buddhism (see page 14) the word *sangha* is used to mean the community of monks and nuns only. Among the first monks were the Buddha's own son, Rahula, and his cousin, Ananda. The monks traveled around India spreading the word and relying on gifts of food to sustain them. They spent the rainy season in monasteries, built by wealthy followers, teaching and meditating.

These young monks in Burma take their begging bowls to be filled with food by the local people in return for a blessing.

## BOY MONKS

In many Buddhist countries, such as Thailand and Burma, young boys often spend several months in a monastery as part of their education. The boys leave home dressed in fine silk clothes and riding on a white horse to imitate Prince Siddhartha before he became the Buddha. When they reach the monastery, they have their heads shaved and put on simple orange robes. While there, they learn about the Buddha and usual school subjects. Some boys go on to become monks; others return to their parents.

Young children dressed in their finery, ready to be initiated as Buddhist monks and nuns before entering a monastery.

Monks taking part in a roof-mending ceremony at a monastery. They ask for the Buddha to bless their work.

## INTERVIEW

I came to the West 20 years ago. I had to leave my monastery in Tibet because I did not agree with the Chinese government. Here, I am able to teach people about the Buddha in calmness and peace.

**Losang Gyatso, age 60**
**Colorado**

## LIFE AS A MONK

Buddhist monks live strict, simple lives, studying the sacred texts and learning to meditate. They also help with the day-to-day running of the monastery, organize festivals and celebrations, and sometimes work with the local community. In countries such as Sri Lanka and Thailand, local people hope to gain merit by putting food in the monks' begging bowls. The monks take the food back to their monastery. This food forms the monks' only meal of the day, and it must be eaten before noon.

### SPOTLIGHT

Monks are allowed to own only eight items, called the Eight Requisites. These were set down by the Buddha himself. They are:
• Saffron, maroon, or black robes
• A begging bowl
• A belt
• A razor
• A needle
• A water filter
• A walking stick
• A toothpick

Part of a monk's day is spent reading and studying the sacred texts of Buddhism, thinking about their meaning.

The grove at Lumbini, Nepal, where the Buddha was born.

## THE BUDDHA'S BIRTHPLACE

The Buddha was born in Lumbini, Nepal. Today, pilgrims can visit a modern temple dedicated to Queen Maya and the pool where she is said to have bathed before giving birth to the Buddha. The ruins of the palace in which Prince Siddhartha spent his early life lie nearby.

## SACRED JOURNEYS

Some of the holiest places for Buddhists are those in India and Nepal where the Buddha was born, gained enlightenment, preached his first sermon, and died. Buddhists come from all over the world to visit these sacred sites.

## ENLIGHTENMENT

The Buddha gained enlightenment under the *bodhi* tree at Bodh-Gaya in eastern India. A descendant of that famous tree still grows on the same spot. Bodh-Gaya is a thriving Buddhist center, with many temples, monasteries, and meditation schools. In winter, the town receives its most famous visitor - the Dalai Lama.

The Buddha was about 80 years old when he died in Kushinagara. The town is now a center for Buddhist pilgrims.

## THE PATH TO NIRVANA

The Buddha preached his first sermon in the deer park at Sarnath in northern India. He died in the small town of Kushinagara in the north-east. A ruined stupa marks the spot where his body was cremated. Inside the Mahaparinirvana Temple in Kushinagara is a huge statue of the Buddha lying on his right side, just as he did when he died.

# SACRED WORDS

Buddhists do not have a single holy book, as Christians have the Bible or Muslims have the Koran. There are 12 sacred texts, some based on the actual words of the Buddha, others on the works of great Buddhist monks and teachers.

## THE THREE BASKETS

For about 400 years after the Buddha's death, his teachings were passed on by word of mouth. Nothing was written down until the 1st century B.C. Then the Buddha's teachings were collected together as the Tripitaka, or "Three Baskets." The first basket contains rules for monks

A monastic library of sacred texts. The books are bound between wooden covers.

and nuns; the second the teachings of the Buddha; and the third an explanation of these teachings. The parts are called baskets because they were originally written on palm leaves that were stored in baskets. The Three Baskets are the main texts of the Theravada Buddhists.

## DIAMONDS AND LOTUSES

The Mahayana school has its own scriptures, called *sutras*. These contain stories and parables to explain difficult points in the Buddha's teachings. Two of the most famous *sutras* are the "Diamond Sutra" and the "Lotus Sutra."

*The Diamond Sutra* was made in China and is the world's oldest printed book.

# THE HARE, THE LION, AND THE EARTHQUAKE

There are many stories about the Buddha appearing in animal form to save the world from harm. This story comes from the *Jatakas*, a collection of stories about the Buddha's life. In it, the Buddha is disguised as a lion.

Once upon a time, a hare was sitting under an apple tree when a dreadful thought struck him.

"What if the Earth fell apart?" he thought. "What would happen to me then?"

At that very moment, a large, ripe apple fell from the tree and landed with a mighty thud right next to the hare. The nervous creature jumped straight into the air. He'd been right all along. The Earth was falling apart! Here was the proof! Without further ado, he turned tail and ran for his life.

As the hare ran, he met another hare.

"Why are you running away?" the second hare asked.

"The Earth is falling apart," came the reply. "Run for your life!" And the second hare ran.

And before very long, behind the first hare ran a hundred thousand other hares, not to mention deer, boars, antelopes, buffalo and rhinoceroses, tigers and elephants.

Then a huge lion appeared.

"Why are you running away?" he asked.

"The Earth is falling apart," they told him. "The hare told us so. Run for your life!"

The lion thought quickly.

"There hasn't been an earthquake in these parts, so what can have startled them? If I don't save them, they will surely plunge into the sea and drown."

He sped to the front of the animals, opened his mouth and roared his great roar, once, twice, then once more. It stopped the animals in their tracks.

"Now, why are you running away?" the lion asked the elephants.

"Ask the deer," came the reply. The lion asked the deer.

"Ask the tigers," they said. And he did.

"Ask the buffalo," they said. And so it went on.

Finally, the lion turned to the hare who had started the panic in the first place.

"Why are you running away?" he asked.

"Well," the hare began, feeling rather foolish. "I was sitting under a tree, minding my own business, when I heard a terrible thud and the Earth began to fall apart around my ears."

Puzzled, the lion set off to investigate. He saw the apple tree surrounded by fallen fruit.

"So, that's it," he thought. "It wasn't an earthquake, it was an apple falling from the tree." Then he ran back to the animals.

"It's safe to return to your homes now," he told them. "The danger is over. I've made sure of that."

And that is how the Buddha, disguised as a lion, saved the animals from a watery fate.

# BUDDHIST FESTIVALS

These Buddhists are celebrating Wesak in Burma by lighting candles.

There are many colorful Buddhist festivals throughout the year. Some are celebrated all over the Buddhist world. Others are local festivals, special to a particular country. Here are some of the most important festivals in the Buddhist year.

### INTERVIEW

At Wesak we clean our houses and decorate them with flowers. We also send cards to each other and give food to the monks. In the evening, we light candles and place them around the statue of Lord Buddha.

Mon, age 9
Bangkok, Thailand

## WESAK

On the night of the full moon in May, Theravadin Buddhists all over the world celebrate the Buddha's birth, enlightenment, and death. This is the festival of Wesak, the happiest and most important day in the year. Statues of the Buddha are decorated with lights to celebrate his enlightenment, and worshipers holding lamps or lighted candles walk around them.

## THE FESTIVAL OF THE GOLDEN TOOTH

The festival of the golden tooth takes place each year, on the night of the August full moon, in Kandy, Sri Lanka. A procession of beautifully decorated elephants parades around the city carrying a golden casket that contains a very special relic - the tooth of the Buddha. This is said to have been snatched from the Buddha's funeral pyre and is normally kept in a nearby temple. The festival is a time of great celebration, with dancing and fireworks in the streets.

A street parade of magnificent elephants carry the Buddha's golden tooth.

## JAPANESE FESTIVALS

Two important Mahayana festivals are celebrated in Japan. The O-bon festival is held in July to honor a family's ancestors. On the first day, families welcome the spirits of their ancestors into their homes. On the second day, there is a great party, with music, dancing, and special food. On the third and final day, families say goodbye to their ancestors and make offerings to the Buddha.

Every year, on May 8, Japanese Buddhists celebrate the Buddha's birth and the coming of spring with the flower festival, Hana Matsuri. In some monasteries, a model is made of the grove of trees in Lumbini where the Buddha was born. There is also a model of a white elephant, to remind people of the elephant who foretold the Buddha's birth.

At the festival of O-bon, Japanese Buddhists remember their ancestors.

Every Buddhist country has its own festivals and celebrations. This festival is taking place in the kingdom of Bhutan.

# GLOSSARY

**bodhi tree** a sacred fig tree.

**bodhisattva** the ideal or perfect person who helps and guides other people toward enlightenment.

**Buddha** someone who has gained enlightenment.

**cremate** to burn a dead body to ashes, instead of burying it in the ground.

**dharma** teaching or faith.

**enlightened** having found the true meaning of life, as if being woken up from a deep sleep and now seeing clearly.

**mandala** a sacred circular design, used to help Buddhists meditate. It may be painted or made of butter or sand.

**mantra** a simple verse that is chanted over and over again to help Buddhists as they meditate.

**to meditate** concentrate very hard and focus your thoughts in order to clear and train your mind.

**missionaries** followers of a faith who travel around the world teaching other people about their beliefs.

**mudra** a special hand gesture seen in statues of the Buddha. Different mudras have different meanings, such as peace, blessing, and protection.

**nirvana** the state of perfect bliss and happiness that all Buddhists try to achieve.

**precept** a rule or guide for how to behave.

**relic** part of a holy person's body or belongings, such as the sacred golden tooth said to have belonged to the Buddha.

**sangha** the worldwide community of Buddhists.

**stupa** a bell-shaped Buddhist shrine.

**sutra** a sacred Buddhist text.

**thangka** a sacred Buddhist painting from Tibet. Different parts of the painting have different meanings.

# INDEX